The Sayings of Jesus

Group and Personal Devotional Bible Studies

by

Peter Willis

MOORLEY'S Print & Publishing
Tel/Fax: (0115) 932 0643

British Library Cataloguing in Publication Data.
A catalogue record for this book is available
from the British Library.

ISBN 0 86071 585 X

MOORLEY'S Print & Publishing
23 Park Rd., Ilkeston, Derbys DE7 5DA
Tel/Fax: (0115) 932 0643

2

CONTENTS

PREFACE

This book comes as a result of a fruitful series of studies shared with the folk at Central Methodist Mission Nottingham. I must point out that I am not a theologian, a biblical scholar or an academic. I am a practitioner in a city centre church. I have no credentials other than my learning, insight and experience in Christian ministry.

I love to share what I know about God and the Christian life, and to do this I have drawn widely on the scholarship of others.

However, I don't want just to teach people *about* God, about the Bible, and so on. I want to drop the preposition in the same way the apostle Paul does in Ephesians 4:20 (RSV), where he speaks of the need for people to "learn Christ", not just learn about Christ.

I am more and more convinced that, both for our current church members and for those we wish to reach, one question is increasingly important: *"Can your church help me experience God and begin a relationship that will transform my life?"* By this question, they're telling us they don't just want to learn about God, they want a transforming relationship with Him. They want to 'learn Christ'.

The Church has well developed structures for teaching information, but we are still quite primitive when it comes to teaching for transformation. The problem is a wonderful God sent opportunity.

My goal in these studies was first to seek to deepen my own relationship with God, then to be a spiritual mentor and teacher seeking to bring others into a transforming relationship too. If these studies help you, as they have helped me, then I have achieved my goal.

Finally, my thanks go to Rev Howard Belben, Rev George Jones and Mr Frank Blackwell. Each one played a vital role in mentoring me into a faith relationship that transformed my life, for which I shall be eternally grateful. My thanks too to Mrs Barbara Grant for her care and skill in proof reading these manuscripts.

Peter Willis

1. NEW BIRTH
John 3: 1 – 21
A PRAYER
Dear Lord, you have loved me from the first
And I thought you did not care.
You always had your arms open to receive me
And I could not see them.
I had thought you far away
Yet you have always been at my side.
I had feared you.
And you've always loved me.
Always there, always caring.
And I did not know.
I thought what I had was all you had given
What I was all you had made,
I dare not believe for more.
I lived with death
While You planned life.
All the time you have loved all that there was
And given all that you had.
Thank you for Jesus.
Through Him you have reached me, at last.
My life, totally changing.
It's like being born all over again.
You have pushed back the boundaries of my life.
Opened up possibilities I could only dream of.
It is as if I have walked from a dark room
Into blazing sunshine.
My whole being, tingling with your presence.
My whole life, teaming with your blessing.
And this is love!
The deepest peace,
A life of glorious wonder.
All this!
Yet, but a hint of what's to come.
Amen.

INTRODUCTION:
In reading the Gospels it is difficult to know where the words of Jesus stop and
the words of the writer of the Gospel begin. They have thought so long about

5

the words of Jesus that unconsciously they drift from them into their own thoughts about them. This makes it difficult to share the sayings of Jesus without sharing the thoughts, beliefs and experiences of the writer. John 3:16 is perhaps the most famous of the sayings of Jesus. However, to understand the saying we must grasp the context. The writer shares with us some important incidents in the life and ministry of Jesus, not in an attempt to give us a life story of Jesus but to pass on particular teaching and truths the writer considers central to the Good News.

1. SO NEAR YET SO FAR (John 3: 1-2)

In writing his Gospel, John is clear who Jesus is. From the very outset to encounter Jesus is to encounter God Himself. John demonstrates the impact of Jesus on individual lives, systems and institutions. He demonstrates that the coming of Jesus is the Incarnation of the Word. John the Baptist witnessed to Jesus as the Lamb of God. Some have recognised Jesus as Messiah and become disciples. At the wedding at Cana, Jesus changes water into wine; it is the first sign that demonstrates the transformation of Jewish religion through the self-offering of Jesus. The cleansing of the Temple has demonstrated the end of the sacrificial system to be replaced in the death and resurrection of Jesus. It is by design, not accident, that the meeting between Jesus and Nicodemus is placed here in chapter three. It is like a staged play that has been carefully choreographed to carry the message. John is sharing with us signs of fundamental change now taking place through the coming of Jesus. Like any writer, John takes us through the drama of discovery, the agony of conflict and decision, but from the beginning he already knows our only logical conclusion.

Nicodemus is a Pharisee. The Pharisees get a very bad press in the Gospels. However, they were some of the best people around. They were the devout Churchgoers of their day, seriously committed to God and His purposes. But in the Gospels we see the Pharisees in the light of their response to Jesus and His teaching. Like the Church today, they were a small group. There were never more than six thousand of them and they pledged themselves to spend all their lives in serving every detail of the scribal law. What did this mean? To the Jew, the Law was the most sacred thing in the world. (First five books in the Bible.) It was the perfect word of God. It contained everything you would need to please God. To keep a good relationship with God you needed to keep the law because it contained all you needed to maintain that good relationship. There are many today who believe this. They claim that if you keep the law and try to live a good life you will be all right. What we experience here is the direct conflict of the Person of Jesus with such teaching.

It is a miracle that Nicodemus overcame his prejudices and his upbringing, to say nothing of his whole view of life, to come to Jesus.

To John, Nicodemus is a representative figure. It is not only Christ and Nicodemus but also Christianity and Judaism, believer and unbeliever, who meet in this encounter. It is structure and faith; Salvation by a system of belief clashing with Salvation through a dynamic relationship with God through Jesus that is represented here.

Here is a man ready to believe in Jesus yet he appears totally incapable of doing so. He keeps all the laws, fulfils all the commands, fits into the system perfectly, he is a good person. Yet he is not sure he has secured eternal life. He is so near, yet so far away. Jesus lays bear the difficulties and brings deeper insight to his and, by inclusion, our plight. In each sentence we are included. At every stage we are compelled to ask what is my position? Where do I fit here?

That all this happens at night is an important symbolic detail. The Jews believed that all the best learning was done at night. Students believe it today. Many of the most meaningful conversations take place late at night. Judaism presumed to already possess the light. To the infant Church, Nicodemus represents someone who comes from that world of darkness into which the true light of God was now shining.

Though Nicodemus came in a genuine spirit, he was not trying in any way to trick or trap Jesus. However, because of his background and upbringing, he would unconsciously assume that he had the right to enjoy the blessings and privileges of the light. No sooner has Nicodemus complemented Jesus than Jesus cuts away all the ground of his security. No-one, Jesus tells him, can experience the reign of God, no matter what his race, degree of piety, dedication of time, devotion of energy, or depth of service. Nothing can clean away the stain we inherit as Adam's seed. The very best of our efforts fall short of the requirement needed to have a sound relationship with God.

2: ONE IMPOSSIBLE HURDLE (3-4)

No Jewish rites, no baptism by John in the Jordan, nothing they could say or do can so change a person's inner life to enable them to live in knowledge and experience of the Kingdom of God. Nicodemus speaks about the miraculous signs which, in his view, make Jesus genuine. Jesus makes it clear that signs and wonders are not the important thing in Kingdom living. He is speaking about a change in the lifestyle of the individual so radical it can only be described as a new birth. Nicodemus thought Jesus was referring to becoming a baby again.

The confusion arises because the Greek for anew is *anothen* and has three meanings:

a: From the beginning, completely radically. Meaning new.

7

b: Again meaning a second time.
     Meaning going back to the beginning.
c: From above. Meaning from God.

Jesus is using the third definition of this word *'anothen'*. To be born anew is to go through such a radical change that it is like being born all over again. This new birth is something not of human achievement, but something coming direct from God.

Nicodemus appears to understand what Jesus is saying only in the second sense, "how can he, an old man, enter again into his mother's womb?" His answer suggests that he is concerned at a level far deeper. Here is a devout man who has tried to do the right thing all his life. He is doing the best he can and still it is not enough. Nicodemus wants to live a life acceptable to God, so securing eternal life. That is why he sought Jesus out, but how? We can empathise with his frustration. He is saying "You speak of this radical fundamental change which is so necessary; but in my experience it is impossible. There is nothing I would like more, but you might as well tell me, a fully grown man, to enter my mother's womb and be born all over again." It is not that Nicodemus does not desire what Jesus offers, it is that he cannot believe it to be possible. Like every person he wants to change, but cannot change himself.

The idea of new birth is basic to the teaching of the New Testament (1 Peter 1:3, 1:22-23, James 1:18; Titus 3:5). It is the same as death followed by resurrection (Romans 6:1-11; 1 Corinthians 3:1,2; 2 Corinthians 5:17; Galatians 6:15; Ephesians 4:22-24; Hebrews 5:12-14). All through the New Testament the idea of rebirth and re-creation is found.

There are four inter-related ideas:
a: Rebirth.
b: Kingdom of Heaven. We cannot enter unless we are reborn.
c: Sonship through adoption.
     This is not possible without rebirth.
d: Eternal Life. Is not possible without rebirth.

To be in the Kingdom of Heaven is to lead a life totally at one with the will of the Father.

To those who believe there is given the power to become sons: John 1:12. Jesus said, "I have come to do the will of my Father." John 14:21. Obedience is the heart and essence of sonship. It is obedience, which does not spring out of a rigid satisfaction of rules and regulations, but out of a living and loving dynamic relationship.

Eternal life is nothing to do with longevity, or duration, but quality. It is the kind of life that God leads. To enter into eternal life is to share the kind of life that God lives. We enter this life through love, reverence, and devotion. All these elements are dependent on, and the by-product of obedience, which springs from love. This is where rebirth fits, that willing acceptance of the free gift of God in Jesus. Rebirth is nothing less than the complete re-orientation of our lives. We liken entry into the Kingdom to physical birth, the emergence from darkness to light, where that which was restricted and confined is at last set free. Many images come tumbling out when we compare New Birth with the movement from the womb into the world: two realms in contrast, the physical material world and the realm of the Spirit.

3: BORN OF WATER AND SPIRIT (5,6)

Nicodemus seems restricted in his knowledge of God to the material, physical realm. But there are two realms; the material, created, physical realm, what Paul calls the realm of the flesh, and the eternal realm, the realm of the Spirit. God's creative power is never limited to the physical and material, Ezekiel 36:25-27. Those who are born again, the new people in Christ, can never restrict God's sovereignty to the natural order. They are born of water, symbol of cleansing which deals with our past. Paul speaks of our going down into the water and dying, then rising to new life in the Spirit. The Spirit enables us to be what, by ourselves, we could never be. Both Water and Spirit stand for the cleansing and strengthening power of God, which wipes out our past and gives us the possibility of victory in the future. Baptism marks out the end of one life, the life of failure and defeat, judgement and death, and the beginning of new life in the Spirit, a life of freedom, communion and victory which is eternally ours in Christ.

4: HE SPEAKS TO ONE AND TO ALL (7-13)

These verses are not just clever prose. Here John lays down a great truth, for this symbolism is fundamental to Christian Faith. The word translated 'wind' can mean both 'wind' and 'spirit'; and the word translated 'sound' can mean both 'sound' and 'voice'. So what John is telling us is… both the **wind** and **the Spirit** blows where **it** or **he** will.

'You hear the sound of **it** or **Him** but you don't know where **it** or **He** comes from or goes to. So it is with every one who is born of the Spirit.' This is John's mechanism for saying to Nicodemus, "This is where you are and this is where you should be." Wind = the physical earthly temporal mystery expressed here when Nicodemus says that he cannot get back into his mother's womb and be born over again, but Jesus, speaking of the Spirit, points to something beyond the physical altogether. However, both hold the same mystery. Jesus is speaking of a spiritual change so radical that it is like being born again. So it is

9

with every one who is born of the Spirit, 3:8. 'Wind' is a word that connects both the terrestrial and spiritual worlds.

Both wind and Spirit can be linked to birth because both are accepted without understanding their origin or destination. However, there is another truth in play here. Neither wind nor Spirit are things we can control. This truth is forcefully evident in birth.

To Nicodemus, eternal life has been something he has sought to achieve through controlled means. In reality it is a gift freely given and freely received. New life in the Spirit cannot be earned, bought or won. Nicodemus is faced with powerful evidence that the Spirit is operating, but has no control of what the Spirit does or how He does it.

In the children's story "The Lion, the Witch and the Wardrobe" the children are speaking with Mr and Mrs Beaver about Aslan. Mrs Beaver said, "If there's anyone who can appear before Aslan without their knees knocking, they're either braver than most or else just silly."

"Then he isn't safe?" said Lucy.

"Safe?" said Mr Beaver; "don't you hear what Mrs Beaver tells you? Who said anything about safe? Course 'e isn't safe. But he is good. He is king I tell you."

In this encounter between Jesus with Nicodemus the old and new clash again. New birth is not won by keeping the law or fulfilling the ritual, but by simply receiving what is offered as a free gift.

This was the testimony of the early church Acts 8:18, 19:6; Galatians 5:22. At this point something very peculiar happens; John changes from the singular to the plural, 3:11. The writer is keen to express not only the witness of the teaching of Jesus of Nazareth, but also the witness of the Risen Christ the Lord Himself, tested and verified in the life and experience of His Body, the Church, 3:11. This is the testimony of those already new-born. It is no longer mere teaching or theory; those who are already alive in the Spirit verify it. It is the writer saying, "We know this is true because we are a living demonstration of this new birth, and we tell you what we have heard and seen and know."

A person either stands in the world of the physical, earthly birth, temporal earth-bound life, living by this world's standards and principles, but doomed to failure, however good or successful; or undergoes a radical transformation and is reborn of the Spirit and enters into the truth, not only of what Jesus teaches, but what Jesus is.

There are two grounds for misunderstanding here:

a: Because we have not reached a stage of experience or knowledge to grasp the truth.

It is no good telling me when I am a six year old what I cannot understand until I am a mature twenty-year-old. There is a journey that has to be made; a process into which the crisis of rebirth fits. Through prayer, love and nurture a person is brought to the place where the Spirit can work and rebirth takes place.

b: Because we are unwilling to understand.
When Jesus Christ comes with His offer to change and re-create us, we simply say; "No thank you: I am quite satisfied with myself as I am and do not want to be changed."

It is easy to sit and discuss and study Christian Faith as a series of academic issues, attend Bible Studies, discuss topics, but the essential thing is to experience Christ for yourself. It is not something that can be understood without experience. A courting couple can spend their evenings together going through books and discussing what falling in love is all about, but eventually one has to put their arms around the other and kiss. Falling in love is not an academic pursuit; it is the experience of an embrace. The inference of verse 13 is that the reality of new birth as the gateway to the Kingdom of God comes, not through discourse or ritual, not through learning or keeping rules, but through an encounter with Jesus Himself. The one who belongs to Heaven has come down to Earth, now known through the ministry of the Holy Spirit, not as an apparition, or dogma, but in the flesh as reality. We can hear from his lips and see in his actions what we could never have discovered, either by striving or learning.

5: OLD TESTAMENT PARABLE (14-15)
John takes an old story from Numbers 21:4-9. The brazen serpent that Moses held up was only a symbol to turn the people's thoughts to God; and when they did they were healed. As Jesus is lifted up people will be drawn to Him and as they believe in Him they too will be healed. This idea of being lifted up relates to both the Cross and to the Ascension of Jesus. The verb to 'lift up' is *hupsoun*. It is used of the cross (John 8:28, 12:32) and the Ascension (Acts 2:33; 5:31, Philippians 2:9). The one could not have happened without the other. The cross is the way to glory as death is to resurrection. So for us, we can, if we like, refuse the Cross that every Christian is called to bear; but if we do, we lose the glory. If there is no cross there is no crown. In the language of Paul, 'unless I die to self, I cannot live in the Spirit. I must become a new creation.'

We have to BELIEVE IN JESUS.
The root meaning of this word believe is 'to put your shirt on something'.
a: To believe that Jesus embodies God and His love for us; his care of us; his desire to forgive and accept us.

b: To believe that Jesus is the Son of God. He has the mind of God, knows the will of God, and is of the same nature as God.

c: To stake everything on Him. Do what He says; obey what He commands; every action done in unquestioning obedience to Him alone. On these beliefs the Church has pinned its very existence. From the first, Christians have been prepared to die rather than deny any one of the fundamental truths of Jesus. Lose these beliefs and you lose real life itself. However, these truths are the fruit of a living relationship with Christ through the ministry of the Spirit, not the mental ascent to a body of doctrine.

Real life is found only in Jesus. It is life in the Spirit, Eternal Life. It is the very life of God Himself. It is not an abstract thing. Life as relating to every minute of every day. I remember working on a building site and being amazed how my fellow-workers would undergo a transformation on Fridays when they got paid. They would be fully alive all weekend, only to die again on Monday morning. To be alive in Jesus is to be fully alive every moment with life abundant. The greatest thing of all is to know that the deepest peace here in this life is only a shadow of that ultimate peace waiting beyond the grave. It is to be fully alive with glorious wonder; pregnant with hope and throbbing with love now; life abundant that will never end.

6: GOD IS FOR REAL (16)

God's love has always been active in our history. God loved and things happened. The writer uses the aorist tense to show this. God loved the world: it is something real and definite to the senses, you can smell it, touch it and taste it, know it intimately.

The magnitude of this love is demonstrated in the uniqueness of His gift. God loved all there was and gave all He had. In this one verse the whole of this dialogue is placed in its eternal context.

In response to such an act of total love, we are challenged to embrace the life that is offered or finally and completely perish! The options are absolute alternatives. Judgement and death are relational; a result of each choice taken now, belief or unbelief chosen now, not in some great assize in Heaven, but now in this world and in this life.

The purpose of His coming demonstrates who the Father is and what He is about in His creation. Light has come into the world (John 1:4, 5, 9). Here the symbols of light and darkness represent the great conflict thrown into focus by the coming of Jesus and now touching every person through the ministry of the Spirit. It is warfare, cosmic in its reach and matter.

There is a battlefield in every individual life; we embrace or hide from the light. The one who embraces the truth about God experienced in Jesus, embraces reality! Here is judgement, that we embrace or run from this reality, reality once and for all clearly seen, as it is revealed in Jesus; known, experienced and appropriated in the Person of Christ through the ministry of the Spirit. Life abundant is embraced or rejected through the choices we make now.

QUESTIONS

1: 'Ready to believe but incapable of believing'. What do you think John Wesley meant in speaking of 'Almost a Christian'?

2: Becoming a Christian. 'A radical fundamental change'.
Does this always have to be so?

3: You cannot change yourself? Why not?

4: Never restrict God's sovereignty to the natural order.
Are you guilty of this?

5: Christianity is not something to be understood but experienced?
Can you only become a Christian when you understand?

6: If you do not own the cross you will never wear the crown. What does this mean in real terms today?

7: Three fundamental issues. What God is like. Who Jesus is. Do I stake my all on Him? Three questions. What do you really believe?
How strongly do you believe it?
What would you give for faith?

8: God loved all there was and gave all He had. Does He love all?
Has He given all in Jesus?

9: Page 10 says, "Our options are absolute alternatives". What do you think that means?

10: Judgement is NOW. It is embracing or running from reality.
How would you explain that to someone outside the Church?

2. SEE ME, SEE THE FATHER!
Matthew 11

A PRAYER
Dear Lord,
I rejoice in the life you have given to me.
I give thanks for the love you have shared with me.
I praise you for the value you have placed on me.
And for the trust you have placed in me.
For in Jesus you have reached down and caught me up into the dynamism of
your creative life.
But Lord, I am fearful:
for I misunderstand your directions so easily.
I misinterpret your word so readily.
I mistake your purpose so frequently.
Often I am protecting so much of yesterday's truth
I fail to make room for your Word for me today.
I am still rejoicing over my work
Still caught up in my action,
Still enjoying my success,
I hold on to so much of you from yesterday
I am in danger of missing you today.
Grant to me such faith that I may recognise you
Not only in what I already know
but in the new experience you now bring.
Grant me such love that I may hold
Not only to the Truth you have given
But the truth you now reveal.
Grant me such obedience
Not only in letting go the old
But in gathering the new.
Grant me such peace
Not in the comfort of where I am
But under the yoke of obedience
That will take me where you want me to be.
Here is my true rest
To find you in my yesterday,
My today and my forever.
Amen.

INTRODUCTION

Up to this point the ministry of Jesus seems to have met with success. The Kingdom has been announced by John the Baptist (Ch 3); and by the words (Ch 5–7) and deeds (Ch 8 & 9) of Jesus, but the Kingdom is not understood or received. Now the atmosphere changes and hostility begins to show itself. Jesus has finished instructing the disciples and He goes, on His own, to teach and preach in nearby towns.

Jesus begins His ministry in Galilee following the imprisonment of John the Baptist. Some suggest that John was imprisoned in a fortress on the east coast of the Dead Sea.

The title in verse two (*ho Christos*) "The Christ" is not incidental. It is the writer's description of Jesus and is the right conclusion we are meant to draw from chapters 5–10. This is an affirmation of 1:17 where the genealogy shows "The Christ" to be the Son of David.

In this Gospel Jesus is King. Wise men come looking for Him who is King of the Jews (2:2). At the triumphal entry into Jerusalem He comes as King (21:1–11). Before Pilate Jesus deliberately accepts the title of king (27:11). Even on the Cross the title is fixed over His head (27:37). In the Sermon on the Mount Jesus quotes the law and five times abrogating it with a regal, "But I say to you...." (5:21,27,34,38,43). The final claim of Jesus is: "All authority is given to Me" (28:18). For Matthew Jesus is the one born to be King. He walks through the pages as if in the purple and gold of royalty.

The true response to Jesus is found in Peter's confession in 16:13-20. Through the various encounters and reactions to Jesus we are led from a view of Jesus as others saw Him to the true confession of His Messiahship which eluded most of His contemporaries, conditioned as they were by false or inadequate ideas of the Messiah.

1: FADED VISION, WRONG IDEAS (1-6)

There appears to be a discrepancy between John's expectations of the coming Messiah, which he had predicted in 3:11 and what he was hearing about Jesus, while in prison. The ministry he was hearing about did not match his understanding (3:11-12). He had fearlessly proclaimed the coming of one who would baptise with fire and whose winnowing fork would separate the chaff to be burned with that fire. Perhaps Jesus was not Messiah after all? The main feature of Jesus' ministry was miracles, which were not a part of John's vision. There were many things about the ministry of Jesus which John could not understand. Could he, a Jew, accept a Messiah who failed to fast (9:14ff)? A Messiah who kept the sort of company John himself would avoid? (9:9ff). He sends his disciples to ask questions.

The question is "Are you the coming one or shall we look for another?" The 'coming one' is a regular term among Jews for the Messiah. The Greek word used for 'someone else' *heteron* suggests that John was expecting a different Messiah (the other word for this is *allos*).

Jesus does not answer directly but uses scripture to meet the challenge to His identity (Isaiah 29:18,19. 35:5-6. 61:1-2). These refer to God's saving work and the mission of His anointed servant. If this did not fit with John's Messianic hopes then he has missed the biblical pattern. There follows a pattern of challenges to the identity and authenticity of Jesus as Messiah (Peter challenged Jesus in speaking of His death, and received a rebuke (16:13-20). Is John offended because Jesus was not doing things he had expected? This is an example, focussed in John, but reflective of a general response to Jesus. John had seen part of the vision but was missing the whole. In what seems a parallel to the temptations, (4:1-11) Jesus again uses scripture to repel a threat to His identity and role. John was not wrong, however, He was looking for the judgement of salvation without the sacrifice which made salvation possible, or the appeal of Divine Love which made response or rejection possible. In this he was no different from others who challenged Jesus' identity as the "Coming One".

In verse 6 many were put off by Jesus, when His style of ministry failed to tally with their expectations, and even offended convention and law. It took spiritual discernment not to be 'put off', or 'tripped up' by Jesus. Those who could accept Him for who He is – are said to be blessed. (This relates to 5:3-10.) While this applies to John's state of uncertainty, it is also a beatitude sharply contrasting John, who represents the many who find Jesus, His ministry and claims, hard to take.

2: SO NEAR YET SO FAR AWAY (7–15)

Jesus demonstrates the importance of John with these three questions. 'A reed shaken by the wind.' John was not a weak, pliable person. It was his rugged independence which attracted such following.

A man dressed in fine clothes? It was a man separate from the establishment, independent in his opinions, unflinching in his judgements. Everything about him points to the role of a prophet. But that is not all.

Verse 10. John is a messenger (Malachi 3:1, Exodus 23: 20). Jesus changes the 'before me' to 'before you', His role is to prepare for the coming of God. Again this is a calm statement so astounding for it clearly implicates Jesus as the coming one.

Verse 11. As Messianic herald John has place of honour. Jesus declares that John is nothing less than the divine herald whose duty and privilege it is to announce the coming of the Messiah. No man could have a greater task than this. Yet he is part of the old order. John is given the task of being a signpost. He points to a new ideal and a new greatness, which others will enter into, but into which he will not come. Many glimpse the glory, labour for it, sometimes die for it, but often never taste the fruit of it. It is not his privilege to be part of the ministry of Jesus, with its new perspective and dynamism.

Verse 12. Now with the ministry of Jesus the Kingdom, which John proclaimed, is already a reality. The violence spoken of here refers to violence inflicted on the Kingdom of heaven. Jesus refers to political activists among John's followers who saw God's mission as a movement for national liberation. Jesus refers to the violent opposition already seen in the arrest and imprisonment of the herald and more ominously seen in the growing official opposition to Jesus Himself. John's suffering was a foretaste of the conflicts which were already beginning to affect the new order. The new Kingdom is already present, a force sufficiently dynamic to provoke violent reaction.

3: THE PROUD AND THE PREJUDICED (16–19)
It is to those who ought to know better that these words are addressed. They attributed John's dour asceticism and judgmental preaching to demonic influence. Jesus came eating and drinking with the outcast, the unrespectable, and they reviled Him as a man given to gluttony, a friend of tax collectors and sinners. Like spoilt children they refuse to play whatever the game was because they cannot have it their way. However God's word comes they will find fault with it; only blind prejudice can explain such behaviour. The ultimate verdict lies not with the cantankerous and perverse critics but with events. John may have been criticized for his eccentricities, but he moved people's hearts to God as they had not been moved for centuries. They might condemn Jesus for mixing with undesirables, but in Him people were finding a new life and a new goodness and a new power to live and a new access to God. To judge by our own prejudices and perversities others who are bringing people to God, even if their methods are not those which suit us, is to miss the wonder of God creating a new thing. However, rejection cannot diminish the evidence or stop the work.

4: MUCH INTEREST NO RESPONSE (20–24)
Most of the ministry of Jesus took place in and around Galilee, in the towns of Korazin and Bethsaida. Capernaum was the centre of all the action. Although the crowds had listened and witnessed the miracles, there had been no serious change of heart – no serious belief. They appear to have rejected John's austerity and failed to see Jesus for who He was. They had great opportunity,

more than any before them, and they had missed it. This is a foretaste of the sorrow of Jesus as He comes to Jerusalem, the "If only you had known (and so received) but now..." The most **rebellious** Babylon; the most **depraved** of sinners Sodom; the most **vicious** of people Tyre and Sidon, would have repented if they had the opportunity that these Galileans had received. Capernaum missed Jesus too because of its **arrogant self-sufficiency.** Arrogance and immorality will be punished, but not as severely as those who reject God's direct appeal. Only the rejection of forgiveness is unforgivable.

5: INNOCENCE THAT SEES AND SIMPLICITY THAT ACCEPTS (25,26)

Those who have set their ways cannot accept the truth about Jesus. God reveals the truth to those who with childlike innocence and openness can receive it. These are the ones the world calls insignificant, but free from false preconceptions, and so open to new light, it is these who become disciples. Prejudice and clever arguments often lead to intellectual and moral blindness. Belief is not the product of natural law, but the gracious will of the Father. It is this revealing will of the Father (1 Corinthians 1:18ff) that brings Spiritual understanding. This does not depend on human equipment or status. His choice falls on those the world would least expect.

6: A TOUCHSTONE TRUTH (27)

This is the most explicit statement of the relationship between Jesus and the Father found anywhere in the Gospels. God has committed to Him all things. The word **'knows'** here means literally to know completely, through and through. There is a unique relationship between the Father and the Son and those He chooses to reveal Himself to. Here again is presented the clear message of who Jesus is. Take it or leave it. There is no other way to know God that is available to humankind. John 14:6. Acts 4:12.

7: AN INVITATION (28–30)

These verses are found only in Matthew. Jesus issues an invitation to all who labour and are heavy laden. This appeal has to be seen in the light of all the opposition we have seen. The uncertainty of John and his disciples who have fixed ideas of what the Messiah must be and do. The leaders who could accept no other Messiah apart from the one that fitted exactly their system of belief. The people who had witnessed so much yet believed so little. To all these Jesus offers a new opportunity. God's appeal is always there. In Jesus He comes always with arms open wide to receive the whosoever.

It is only by taking up the yoke of Christ that you find rest. The yoke is, in the Old Testament, a symbol of submission (Isaiah 9:4; 58:6; Jeremiah 27-28 also 2:20). The invitation reminds us of 23:4 where the Scribes and Pharisees are charged with making the people carry heavy loads through legalistic demands. Faith was meant to honour God, but the leaders had developed a faith which had condemned ordinary people to hard labour. Sometimes our attempts to impose faith brings weariness because belief that is learned, becomes an intolerable burden. It is not meant to be like this Jesus is saying. The yoke that Jesus speaks of is a way of life which springs from love, a way of gentleness and humility. The Greek for easy *(chrestos)* means fits like a favourite old jumper, so the word here can mean well-fitting so we can read, "My yoke fits so easily that my burden is light." It is not 'obedience to the letter of the law' but a response to a living person. This is counter to the yoke of the law which is strict obedience to all the precepts and commandments.

The yoke of Jesus is easy, not because it makes lighter demands, but because it means entering into a loving relationship (learn of me). The meaning here is better translated "Learn from me **that** I am gentle and humble in heart." This is the lesson that leads to rest of spirit and soul. Although the demands of the Kingdom are great (5:17-20), they appear in a different light when seen as expressions of loving obedience, rather than demands for religious achievement. The promise of rest for your souls brings us sharply again to the content of the chapter and the failure of the people to respond to Jesus. It is a quote from Jeremiah 6:16, an offer to follow His way; to those who do, He issues an invitation to use His name. Where love is recognised, obedience becomes a loving response. Again we could conclude that where there is obedience then the yoke is easy. The yoke is hard when there is no submission.

QUESTIONS

1: What do you find difficult about Jesus?

2: Few finish well. Why do you think this is?

3: Why does Jesus and His message of the Kingdom provoke so much violent opposition?

4: Verses 16–19 We danced and you would not join in. Is this true today? How?

5: Christianity is not something to be understood but experienced. How does this fit in with being a witness?

6: There were many followers but few disciples. Is there a difference?

7: Share examples of unbelief you have experienced. How would you respond?

8: Make a list of your Church's principles and practices. How much is yours and how much is essential to the Kingdom?

9: What are the things that keep you from wholehearted obedience to Jesus?

10: How far has the Church made faith a burden?

11: 'My yoke is easy'. Yet the demand of Jesus is to total self-sacrifice – How do you explain this?

12: In verses 20-24, harsh judgement is given because of the measure of opportunity received. If this is so, where do you stand?

3. THE OLD AND NEW IN CONFLICT
John 5

A PRAYER

Dear Lord,
Again and again you have opened a window
And in the most astounding and amazing ways
You have reached into my ordinary life
Touching, teaching, transforming,
Refreshing and renewing me, I am so blessed.
But in holding on to what I have already received,
I miss so much of what you desire to give.
I have grasped your anger
and missed your forgiveness.
I have seen your judgement
and missed your mercy.
I have experienced your power
but missed your humility.
I have understood your law
but missed your love.
Help me not to hold so tightly
to yesterday's knowledge
that I miss today's revelation.
to formulate yesterday's direction
that I miss today's truth.
To encapsulate yesterdays experience
that I miss today's fresh encounter.
Save me from making things so important
that I fail to value the people around me.
Making laws which keep me in, but puts them out.
Holding rules that give me privilege,
but make them subservient.
Enforcing principles that give me pride,
but which destroys instead of bringing them life.
Lord, keep me alert and alive to you.
Always ready to give up what I had yesterday
in exchange for all you offer today.
Amen.

INTRODUCTION:

The New Testament has much to say about the refusal of the Jews to accept Jesus as the Messiah (Luke 19:41-44). Paul also expresses this conflict in his heart-wrung confession found in Romans 9:2,3.

John's Gospel has sometimes been called "The Gospel of the rejection." The Gospel was written in Ephesus in about A.D. 100. For John, Jesus brings reality into a world of shadows and imperfections. John saw the events of Christ's life not simply as happenings in time; he saw them as windows opening onto eternity. It was a reality which had been entombed in Jewish law and ritual but was now, through Jesus, set free.

Another great issue at the time of John's writing was the rise of heresy within the new Church. The temptation has always been to begin with faith and then continue with a system or structure. This temptation came not only through continuing Jewish pressure, but also from Gnostic influence. The Gnostics had a system of belief which held the idea that the created world was evil, totally separated from, and in opposition to, the spiritual world. They concluded that God the holy, dwelt in unapproachable isolation and in perfect splendour. He had no dealings or contact with creation. God the holy had delegated responsibility for creation to a minion. The creator was an inferior being who kept humans imprisoned in material existence, isolated from the spiritual world and without any hope of ever being part of it. For the Gnostic, trying to get to God was like trying to contact the chief executive in the Local Authority and being continually passed from one minor official to another. You could never get to God. Only those who had the 'divine spark' had any hope at all. To escape they needed 'enlightenment' (knowledge = 'Gnosis') which was brought to them by a divine redeemer who comes from the spirit world in disguise. For the Gnostic salvation is a matter of self-realization. The Gnostic denied the historical events of the life, death and resurrection of Jesus. Jesus could not possibly have been human or pre-existent. To counter the Gnostics and their strange system of belief, John presents a Jesus who is undeniably human and yet undeniably divine. This was blasphemy to the Jews and an anathema to the Gnostics. In this major slice of John's material, the writer attacks these sterile systems of institutional belief.

Chapter five begins with an account of a mighty work of Jesus; and in each case the evangelist is relating stories similar to those found in the earlier Gospels. All four Gospels record the passion of Jesus in a Passover setting. It is under the shadow of the Passover that this great controversy takes place. Jesus reveals Himself as the Living Bread which came down from Heaven, and promises that all who eat the Bread will live forever. He then adds the words which are so offensive to the Jews and Gnostics alike, 'And the bread that I will

24

give is my flesh, which I will give for the life of the world' (6:51). Whatever else may be involved in the controversies between those who believe in Jesus and those who disbelieve in Him, it is in their attitude to His death that their belief, or disbelief, most conspicuously shows itself. This was true during His earthly life and has been true ever since. To believe in Jesus is to enter into a dynamic and intimate relationship with the Divine.

1. A SIMPLE ENCOUNTER? (1–9)

This is a simple story until you begin to recognize the politics behind the words and images. The pool at Bethzatha means place of the olive. (We used to call this Bethesda meaning place of mercy.) It was situated south of the temple in the valley of Kidron. This then is the setting in which Jesus heals the lame man.

Every incident in John's Gospel fits together to build the message the writer wants to convey. Each story strengthens the argument and adds power to the message.

In the story of the wedding feast (John 2) water was turned into wine. Water is symbolic of the Jewish rite of cleansing. Jesus turns the water into wine demonstrating clearly that his own sacrifice would replace, once and for all, the sterile Jewish rite of purification, the wine being symbolic of the Last Supper in which He declares, "This is my blood of the new covenant!" This conflict between the cleansing rites of the Jewish faith and the cleansing blood of Jesus is reminiscent of the old Gospel song "Are you washed in the blood of the Lamb?". For John this miracle is a direct challenge to the old order of ritual cleansing.

Again in His encounter with the woman at the well (John 4), Jesus makes it clear that He provides the 'water' that quenches the deepest thirst once and for all. The challenge here contests that the old order, represented by the well dug by Jacob, which never satisfies and which demanded constant visits, is passing and is to be replaced by the new order in which He himself satisfies spiritual thirst by indwelling the believer, like a well springing up within them.

In this encounter at Bethzatha when water is used as a means of healing, Jesus demonstrates that He, not the old order, is the true healer. We are told that the pool had five porches and it is hard not to make the link with the five books of the law through which Jews were to find wholeness of life. The many sick who gathered each day around the pool demonstrated clearly that the old order had failed. The man in this story represented the whole nation. Jesus speaks to this man whose disability made it unlikely or impossible for him ever to be first into the pool. This man had been coming to the pool for thirty-eight years.

Thirty-eight years is exactly the number of years Israel wandered in the wilderness waiting for the promise of God to be fulfilled (Deut 2:14). John is telling us, with stunning force, that the old system is impotent and ineffective. Jewish faith is powerless to help the sick; it is merely empty rites and rules. This then is not simple a story of the healing of a lame man. It is a confrontation between two conflicting realities. We are experiencing the barrenness and sterility of the Mosaic Law in Jewish tradition and the alienating structures of Gnostic thought in conflict with the quickening, life-giving Word of Jesus.

a) Jesus asked the man if he wanted to be cured. It was not such a stupid question as it appears and it is just as relevant now as then. After thirty-eight years and so many disappointments expectancy dies, hope disappears and apathy takes over. His daily visit to the pool has become a matter of habit, a daily routine of being carried to the pool, meeting friends and passing the time of day. Nobody expected anything to happen. Jesus addresses His question through the sick man to the Jews and Gnostics, answering before God – did he want to be healed? Was he really satisfied with what the old order was delivering to him? Whatever else the Jewish or Gnostic systems offered the lame man, the question remained. Did he want to be healed? Before you can receive the power Jesus offers, you must desire it and believe it possible. If you are satisfied with what you have, God cannot give you anything new. Here is where the conflict between the old and new resides. If you stay where you are in whatever old order is yours, there can be no hope for you.

b) You must take the risk and allow desire to blossom into action. It is as if Jesus said to this man, "Your desire and My power together can change your life forever." The power of God never dispenses with your freedom. Like the lame man, you must face your own helplessness. When your will and God's power co-operate miracles happen.

c) Having told the story of the miracle, John adds, almost as a footnote, that it took place on the Sabbath. This comment must have sent the Jews and Gnostics into a screaming rage and pushed the controversy over the edge of reason.

2: HEALING BRINGS HATRED (10–18)

The scene switches; the man is now healed and is walking home, carrying his bed under his arm. He is stopped by the authorities who tell him he has broken the law. Perhaps he is so intoxicated with his new lease of life given to him by Jesus that he has forgotten the rules of the old order. The man is suddenly caught up in the conflict between the Jews, Gnostics and Jesus. We see the power of the new order at work; Jesus gives His orders, and in obedience to His word, power comes. Now, confronted by the authorities, all the man can say is

'The man who healed me said to me, "Take up your bed and walk"' (5:11). He can only point to Jesus! He has no theology, no religious structure, and no system of belief. All he can say is, "this man told me to take my bed home". John shows us that it is the man's experience of Jesus which matters, not adherence to a system of belief. Only later does John record Jesus as saying to the man, "See you are well again. Stop sinning, or something worse may happen to you" (5:14). The miracle that brings wholeness is not simply a mechanical thing.

Climbing into the pool represents the old order, getting in first secures healing. In the new order, life and wholeness are not automatic, but relational. New life and wholeness are only possible within a living relationship with Jesus. John makes clear to us that health is not maintained by keeping rules or fulfilling rites, but through maintaining a real relationship with Jesus. Unless the man develops his relationship with the Son, he will expose himself to an invasion of a demonic kind that will be worse than before.

a) V.15: Being in relationship with Jesus brings the believer into conflict with the old order. You should never expect a quiet life when you get to know Jesus. This man meets Jesus, is healed and the first time he uses his legs he is arrested. He gains use of his legs and is in danger of losing his life. The penalty for breaking the Sabbath rules was death by stoning. The man tries to explain that it was not his fault that he had broken the law. The verbs in v.18 are imperfect tense, describing repeated actions in the past. This incident was only a sample of what Jesus habitually did; to know Jesus was to get into trouble.

b) The defence Jesus gave was staggering, "My Father is always at His work to this very day, and I, too, am working" (v.17). The old order is affronted again. The Jewish leaders had reasoned that God rested from creation but still did works of judgement, mercy, compassion and love. What offends the Jewish leaders is not the idea that God worked on the Sabbath, maintaining moral standards and putting right the wrongs of creation, but when Jesus claims, "I am working too." He is claiming a special place in relation to the Father. Compared with this claim, the charge of Sabbath-breaking is a minor difficulty. For the Gnostics, He dares to suggest that God and man can be in relationship or, worse, work together. Here we see clearly the conflict between a system of belief and personal experience of the unique Power behind the system. For Jesus, personal experience and relationship are at the heart of real belief.

c) Verse 18: the phrase 'His Father' is better translated 'His very own Father'. This was a direct insult to both Jew and Gnostic alike. Jesus, they claimed, was making Himself equal to God. For the Jew, it was blasphemous because it was tantamount to claiming to do what God alone could do. For the Gnostic, it was blasphemy because it was claiming an intimacy with God which, for them, was not possible. Here John is claiming that the incarnation is neither the Father nor the Son acting independently, but the Father and Son acting together. 'God in Christ reconciling the world'. In the same way Paul speaks of the disciple's actions as "Christ in me".

d) For the Jewish leaders sin and illness were bound up together. In healing the man Jesus had in reality forgiven his sin. That Jesus told the man to sin no more only added fuel to the fire. The charge of blasphemy was inevitable. The new order was under attack. The challenge is clear; if you accept words like these then you either accept Jesus as divine Son of God or condemn Him as self-deluded blasphemer.

3: ONE CLAIM TOO FAR (19–29)

In His defence Jesus claims that He is the very opposite of a rebellious son. His is one with the Father a oneness in which there are neither Father actions nor Son actions, but only actions which both Son and Father share. Here again we see a sharp contrast between the new order of Jesus and the old order of the religious authorities. On the one hand a relational experience which brings life, on the other a commitment to the letter of the law which does not rely on any relationship with the Father and because it has become divorced from Him now kills.

Verse 19 is of great importance because it summarises John's understanding of Jesus. For John it is not the rites and demands of the old order by which heaven is brought to earth and made real in human life and history, but through the coming of the Son (1:51).

a) Verse 20: On the surface they have just witnessed the healing of a sick man; but in reality what they have seen is only the preamble to what God is about in their presence. John reveals the full truth of incarnation reality as a composer builds a piece of music. Already we have met Nicodemus, who had fulfilled all that the commandments required, but still looked to secure eternal life. Keeping the commandments had not secured eternal life. Jesus tells Nicodemus that he needs to be born again. He promised the woman at the well, "water welling up within her, bringing eternal life." John is building the crescendo to the moment when Jesus will not only give new life to a living man, but to one who has been in the tomb three days (John 11:38-44). John will not stop until the crescendo reaches its peak when the body of Jesus Himself will lie in the tomb and then be raised by the greatest work of the Father in the Son.

b) Verse 21: Jesus states that through the unique, exclusive and divine prerogative He shares with the Father – He gives life to whom He wills. Nobody is fully alive except in relationship with Jesus.

c) Jesus is now the touchstone by which everything is tested; how you react to Him determines life and death (v.22).

d) For John, Jesus brings unquenchable hope and unconquerable certainty. You may be persecuted and disregarded, small in number and dogged by poverty, totally without human influence. The early Church faced failure and disloyalty but never doubted the ultimate triumph of Christ. The old order may delay God's purpose but it can never defeat it (v.23).

e) In the new order, to accept Jesus brings life, to reject Him brings death. It means strength for all that accepting him involves. To follow Jesus changes mystery into intimacy, fear into love, selfishness into service and enmity into forgiveness. Weakness becomes strength; frustration turns to achievement; and tension to peace (v.24).

4: FROM THE OLD TO THE NEW (25–29)

Here again Jesus confronts those who hold on to worn-out systems of belief that cannot deliver the promises they make. Jesus claims He, the Son of Man, is the life giver, He will raise the dead to life and then judge them according to their lifestyle. John is pointing to two kinds of death, Spiritual death and physical death and, in doing so, contrasts vividly the old and the new. A system of belief that cannot deliver, burdens believers and creates spiritual decline.

a) Apathy comes through the back door as hope leaves through the front door. When your spirit is beaten and goals are placed out of your reach, failure is all-consuming and you find it easier to give up than to keep trying. When you stop trying you invite spiritual death.

b) The absence of feeling is also a sure sign of impending death. To have become insensitive to what is happening around you is to be spiritually dead. The Gnostics and the Pharisees were so committed to their religious structure and belief they had lost the ability to feel any empathy with those around them. You can look evil in the face and feel no indignation. You can be confronted with sorrow and suffering and feel no grief or pity. But to lose compassion is to lose the very spark of life itself.

c) You say, 'to prolong life you must keep the mind active.' When you stop thinking you invite death. When your mind becomes so closed that it cannot face the challenge of new truth, and the desire to learn is lost, then spiritual death is not far away.

d) When you stop feeling the pain of a wrong and the desire to repent you invite spiritual death. The day you sin in peace is the day you die spiritually. Only the one who experiences a close relationship with Jesus can hope to live. Jesus makes clear that what happens to us beyond death is totally bound up with what we do before death.

5: HIS JUDGEMENT ALONE IS TRUE (30)

Jesus claims that He alone has the right to judge others. This is the most direct challenge yet to religious leaders who, through their piety, rituals and rules, had claimed for themselves the authority to judge others. Doggedly holding to a system of belief and practice that, by its nature, excluded the majority of ordinary people and made any relationship with God the exclusive right of the few, their judgement of Jesus comes from injured pride, blind prejudice, bitter jealousy and arrogant contempt. It was harsh and intolerant. It was judgement corrupted by self-righteousness and affected by self-conceit; judgement that was based on envy, insensitivity and ignorance. All this was clearly exposed by the presence of Jesus who, being one with the Father, knows the standards, is loving, true and full of knowledge to understand people and their circumstances. The claim of Jesus to judge is founded on His claim that He bears in His body God's nature. He emphasises His total lack of independence, He and the Father are in complete unity. He is seeking only to please the Father who sent Him.

6: ACCEPTABLE WITNESS? (31–36)

Jesus agrees with the challenge of His accusers that any witness which is not verified by others is not acceptable. He points to John the Baptist (1:19,20,26; 1:29,35,36) as a human witness able to stand in His defence. He pays tribute to John as a shining light, v.35. The function of light is to point the way, and John was still pointing the way to God and to whom Jesus was. However, the Jewish leaders did not recognise John as God's messenger. He was a passing interest, to be tolerated as long as he said what they liked to hear, abandoned and opposed when he began to be an irritant. However, Jesus did not need John's evidence; He looked to the highest and greatest witness of all. He claimed that the witness of the works themselves were the greatest evidence of the power of God working through Him. His supreme witness is God. It is said of great artists that they should never explain their art, it should speak for itself. The messengers of God never need to justify their witness, it has its own power of persuasion and its own defence. His accusers had thought to discern God in the words, but had forgotten that He is known primarily through his actions. He is a God not to be encountered in abstract thought, but through His active involvement in our history

7: THE CHIEF WITNESS (37–43)

The witness of John, the witness of the works, the witness of God Himself, all point to three things Jesus speaks of here. Hearing God, seeing God, having the Living Word dwell within, are all central to the bedrock teaching of the Jewish scriptures. The old order has produced none of these things. To the Jew, the scriptures were all in all. They believed that to know the words of the law was to gain eternal life (remember Nicodemus). They searched and knew the law and still did not receive God. They read with closed minds. You can read the Bible in such a way that will bolster your opinions, find authority for intolerance, support your ideology and affirm your set rules, rather than discover God's will and authority at work around you. They made an even bigger mistake – they thought they had a written revelation of God, complete and leather-bound. Their mistake bound them to worshipping a God others had seen, a God others had met, a God active only in other people's history. They could only grasp what He had done. He was no longer the 'I AM' doing a new thing, actively redeeming the present age. They completely missed God active and living among them. When you hang on to who God was and what God did yesterday, you can so easily miss Him today. Jesus is not arguing to score points, or to beat down His opponents, never to win applause, but to reveal the Father. In this confrontation the flame that burns brightest is that of love.

8: MEASURES FOUND WANTING (44–47)

The old order, with its strict rules and regulations, bound God to the past. The leaders had built such a vast edifice of restrictions and carefully detailed structures to belief that only experts could participate. Faith became accessible only to the professional. Religion can, through its language, dress and activity, imprison God, making any access to Him impossible for the majority of ordinary people. For the elite and well-educated, the privileged and the informed it became a matter of prestige, something to take pride in; for the favoured it bred a desire for the praise and the servitude of others. So long as we measure ourselves against those around us we will be satisfied. I remember my father being ill. Before the doctor arrived he thought that he was at death's door. The doctor referred him to hospital and I remember our first visit. "How are you?" I said. To my amazement he said, "Oh I'm really doing very well! Certainly better than that man over there, he's very sick. He won't be with us much longer."

We can always find someone in a worse position than we are, who will, in comparison, make us look better. Comparison with others kills faith. I only know how healthy my faith is, or how strong my relationship with God is as I look to Jesus. Looking to Jesus, I have no hope in myself, in my circumstances or my reputation and at that moment faith is born.

Verse 45: Jesus gives a charge that strikes at the very root of both Judaism and Gnosticism. The religious leaders in Judaism placed their hope in their understanding of the books Moses had given them, believing them to be the true words of God. They had encapsulated the law and thought that their strict adherence to the law of Moses would be their protection. Jesus declares that the very law they claim for defence will be the judge that condemns them.

Taking, interpreting and trying to live by the rules, they thought they had understood Moses and gained favour with God, but they failed to understand the purpose of the law. The purpose of the law was to forge a living relationship with a living God, a relationship which should have led them to recognise Jesus, but they did not see that all that Moses had written pointed to Jesus. Had they believed Moses, they would have believed Jesus.

The Gnostics thought they had been given special knowledge. Certainly if they were given the knowledge, they had failed to use it. Responsibility is always the flip side of privilege. They had become so wedded to a system of belief that they could not accept the God behind their system. No system of belief, no structure of law, no high dedication to sacred ritual can save sinners or secure eternal life. God alone is holy, He alone has knowledge and He alone is loving enough to be able to judge without flaw or favour. Moses pointed to Jesus who made the truth transparent, love accessible and forgiveness and acceptance available to all. Still today the choice is ours. To choose Jesus is to choose change and encounter trouble.

QUESTIONS

1: Sterile religion can so disappoint that expectancy dies, hope disappears, and apathy takes over.
What do you think?

2: The Power of God never dispenses with our freedom! What do you think this means?

3: The first essential to receiving the Power of Jesus is to desire it. Is this true?

4: Creeds and religion are the enemy of living Faith? 5:11.

5: Healing is not a physical thing, it is relational? 5:14.

6: Nobody is fully alive except in Jesus? 5:21.

7: How true are verses 25–29? Notes 4: a,b,c,d.

8: Do we have any right to judge others? 5:30.

9: How important are the witness of works?

10: Does self-satisfaction kill faith?

11: You can read the Bible to bolster your opinion, rather than discover God's will. How do we do this?

12: They worshipped what God had done and missed what He was doing! How do we stop doing this?

4. GETTING ALONG TOGETHER!

Matthew 18

A PRAYER

Dear Lord,
I bow in your presence words spent,
Argument silenced,
Resistance shattered,
Will broken, Wealth gone,
Self-sufficiency in tatters.
A debtor to your love.
Shamed, for I have offended you
And the debt of my offence defies measurement.
Were I to own the spread of heaven I could not pay.
Were I to reap all the wealth of the earth
I could not redeem the wrong.
I bow in your presence
Overwhelmed by your Grace.
For you have cleared the debt.
You have set me free.
You have turned my understanding upside down.
Turned the reasoning of my world mad,
It's seeing blind.
It's feeling numb.
You have brought me low. I am a child again.
Learning with fresh excitement
To think and see, feel and touch.
A new life, driven by your Grace.
I am a child again
learning to relate to those around me;
Faltering steps of forgiving love.
I am a child again
Sharing a new honesty that tells the truth in love.
A new humility that counts others better than me.
In your presence, rejoicing
For you have given me a new family.
Best of all you have brought heaven within my reach,
through Jesus.
Amen.

INTRODUCTION:

This is the fourth major collection of Jesus' teaching in Matthew, which is concluded by the formula in 19:1. It is teaching not just for the twelve, but for all disciples. The writer is concerned with relationships among the followers of Jesus. Belong to any church today and you will immediately recognise the need for such teaching. Within the community of the believers there is always ample opportunity to both harm and help others. The health and effectiveness of the group will depend on their attitude to one another. We are presented with the needs of a developing church. You could call this chapter Matthew's Pastoral Guide to Relationships.

1: UPSIDE-DOWN VALUES (1–5)

The passage begins with an academic question which comes out of the disciples increasing awareness of who Jesus is (17:25–26). If Jesus has a special relationship with the King of Heaven, then how do the authority structures of the new Kingdom of Heaven relate to structures here on earth? This is not a question focussed on some grand vision but on personal relationships; who is boss and who is servant? How do we relate to one another? It is not a question about individual importance, still less about a personal pecking order. Human society takes rank and authority very seriously. How are these issues to be treated in this new society? How will the new order function? What is citizenship in the new order all about?

The answer Jesus gives is mind-blowing for it totally reverses all human values. To demonstrate this, Jesus takes a little child and stands it at the centre of the group. A child had no standing in Jewish Society, not to be taken seriously except as a responsibility.

If you are aiming at the fulfilment of personal ambition, the gaining of personal power, the enjoyment of personal benefits, high reputation and standing, then the Kingdom of God is not for you. In this teaching every principle of an earthly kingdom is turned on its head. True greatness in the Kingdom of God is to be found in everything that is opposite to earthly kingdoms. The Kingdom demands the denial of self, the reckless spending of self through a life of service and sacrifice, working for others, not gaining for self. True greatness was to be found in being little, true importance in submissiveness. All this relates not to a trait in character but a change in position. The writer is not urging the disciple to become childlike. Paul wants to treat the church members like mature adults, but they are behaving like unruly children, demonstrating immaturity in church. This kind of childishness is not what Jesus is getting at. (Phil. 2:8. The same phrase is used, compare 1 Cor. 3:1). The little child has three great qualities:

a) Innocence: In relating to individuals or the crowd children have no hidden agendas but their actions and attitudes are transparent.
b) Dependence: Children are completely reliant on those who love and care for them.
c) Trust: Children never doubt the ability or wisdom of those who make promises. These are the very qualities which counted for everything in the context of the new Kingdom.

There is a movement of thought which begins in verse 5. The 'child' in verses 2–4 = insignificant believers of verses 6, 10, 14. 'One such child' does not refer to children but to the disciple who accepted the child's status. Their greatness lies in their relationship to Jesus.

2: WATCH YOUR FEET! (6–9)
These verses are linked together by the Greek words *skandalizo* = cause to sin (6, 8, 9) and *skandalon* = temptation (three times in v.7) the root word for scandal. These words form an important part of Matthew's presentation. The idea here is one of being tripped up. It reminds me of working in a clothing outfitter's and watching children sliding on the freshly cleaned and polished floor. One older staff member used to stand at the end of the counter and stick out his foot just as the child was sliding past. The child would go sprawling along the floor and the assistant would rush out and grab the screaming child saying how dangerous sliding on polished floors was. *Skandalon* is one person tripping another up. Being 'tripped up' is a real danger for all disciples, especially those young in the faith, which does not relate to years but to maturity. You can be young in the faith as easily at eighty as eighteen. Disciples are vulnerable both from one another, verses 8, 9, and from members of an unbelieving community, verses 6, 7. One can be tripped up as much by a disparaging attitude, a lack of concern or pastoral oversight. Tripping up another disciple can be an action consciously or unconsciously done, or a word knowingly or unknowingly spoken. A refusal to forgive is as dangerous as a direct temptation to sin.

The language changes from 'child' in verse 2–4 to 'little ones'. Each refers to disciples (similar language is used of the disciples in 10:42, 11:25, and it will appear again in the 'least' of these 25:40, 45). The disciples appear in the word's eyes to be weak, insignificant and vulnerable, poor in spirit, meek and persecuted (5:3-12). Though what is said applies to new disciples, it also applies to all who are part of the Christian community. Anyone who trips a fellow disciple, by attitude or action, or even by failure to act, is so severely dealt with, that a quick drowning would be merciful. It would seem that the punishment is out of proportion to the crime. "It would be better…" might suggest simply that it would be better for them and Him, to be rid of him.

Verse 7 accepts that the *'scandala'* is part of this world system. The Christian will be vulnerable until the Second Coming. There can be no dropping of our guard until He comes or calls. It stresses the importance of example and the terror of leading another to sin. It emphasises the punishment that awaits those who lead others to sin. (Donkey stone was a mill stone too large to be turned by hand.) It makes clear that this is a dangerous world and marks the responsibility each Christian has for the well-being of another. In every part of their life the disciples must be careful and watchful. Certain things may be of no threat whatsoever to them personally, but deadly to those around them. Once and for all we are clearly taught that we are our brother's keeper. Paul in his teaching on what to eat and drink says "I can, but I don't because I am answerable for my weaker brother and sister."

Verse 8–9: There are two senses in which this passage can be taken. **First:** Personally, it is worth any sacrifice and any self-renunciation to escape the punishment of God. **Secondly:** You can take it in connection with the Church. The whole passage is about those in the faith who are vulnerable. If there is someone whose self-life and conduct is damaging the Body of the Church, they must be rooted out and cast away. The Church is the Body of Christ; if that Body is to be healthy and health-giving, all that threatens its health must be surgically removed, however painful it my be. If we allow it to stay it will destroy the whole Body. This passage stresses both the necessity of self–renunciation for the Christian individual and discipline for the Christian Church. Sometimes we have abdicated our responsibility for each other both by our refusal to set clear standards and our failure to be living examples of the faith we claim. The severity of the punishment highlights the vital importance of personal behaviour. Amputation is extreme, but the writer is suggesting that it is better to have no hands than fail another. There could be no sharper emphasis placed on the Christian's lifestyle than what you do, say, and are in relation to those around you. Just as important is the way each individual affects the whole body. We know in personal hygiene that any impurity can infect a member and make the body sick. My dear disciple, your sin diminishes me and my sin weakens your witness, so bound together is the Body of Christ that there must be no personal sacrifice too costly to maintain the health of the whole.

3: LITTLE IS BIG TO GOD (10–14)

The welfare of those considered to be unimportant by the world is of constant concern to God. One mention of their guardian angels tells us that God is intimately aware of every single individual. For any to consider even one to be beneath their concern is to violate God's divine intention (Hebrews 1:14).

The importance of every single individual is also emphasised in the parable of the sheep. This parable is addressed to the disciples. It reminds them that God's pastoral care is inclusive of all (Luke 15). The sheep here are not lost, only astray, separate from the Father who loves them.

Verse 14: The disciple is to share the concern of God for all the 'little ones' and neglect none. It shows the Love of God to be:-

a: Personal love: He cannot be happy until the last child is safe home.

b: Patient love: people may be foolish and irresponsible, but His love does not waver. He loves even the one who has only himself to blame for his sin and sorrow.

c: Persuing love: God comes looking for the lost.

d: Praising love: It is pure joy to God when one returns home.

e: Protecting love: makes the wanderer wise, the weak strong, the sinner pure, the captive free. This parable is a lesson for the disciple on how to share the Father's intimate concern for the wandering sheep. All are only strayed, it is the task of the disciples to make sure that not one is lost (Isa. 53:6).

4: APPROPRIATE ACTION (15–20)

This word is addressed not to the Church but to individual disciples (you singular). The concern is not to punish an offender but how to rescue a fellow disciple who is not only endangering their own life but the life of the whole Church. The concern here is how the disciples will react to a personal offence made against them, not a breakdown in relationship. It is about repentance, not restitution.

As a first principle, the disciple must not ignore the fault in his brother or sister. To ignore this principle is to risk damaging the whole Body. You must confront them with it, in the hope that they may repent (1 Cor. 9:19-22; 1 Peter 3:1). Pastoral concern can easily degenerate into a destructively critical spirit. What Jesus is saying is simply, "If anyone sins against you, spare no effort to make that person admit their fault and to get things right again between yourself and the offender." Never tolerate a situation in which there is a breach of personal relationships between you and another member of the Christian community. The purpose here is to restore fellowship with a brother or sister. The reason for this teaching is not so that you can prove that you are right, not for reparation, for easing your feelings, or getting something off your chest. Sadly this passage is one least obeyed by Christians today. What do we do? We talk, or we bury it deep and refuse to forgive. You cannot simply disregard it, that is to add to the wrong. What are we supposed to do to put it right? It is your spiritual duty to speak to him or her.

1: Put the complaint in words. Bring it out into the open.

2: Speak to the brother or sister personally and privately. There is only one way to settle things and that is face to face. Make it a matter between you and that person alone.

3: If a personal approach fails to get results, take the advice of Deuteronomy 19:15. If they refuse to listen, take one or two others. There is a link here in thought with the Promise of Jesus found in verse 20. The matter is no longer personal but threatens the very life of the Body.

4: If that still fails, we must take the matter to the Church fellowship. Why? Because it is often only in the atmosphere of Christian prayer, love and fellowship that personal relationships can be made whole.

5: When every effort fails it looks as if Jesus commands us to abandon the wrongdoer as worthless. Jesus cannot have meant this. He never sets limits on forgiveness. It is not a command to abandon, but a challenge to win him with the love that can touch even the hardest life. It is not a statement marking hopeless cases, but a declaration that Christ insists that there is no such thing as hopeless people and insists that we do not give up on anyone. We must recognize that this break in relationship is no longer personal but must be handed over to Jesus.

6: **Verse 18:** There is a change to the plural tense here. The appeal in verse 17 is the second principle, based on the Church's united conviction of what is the right and wrong conduct for a disciple. This is vital. Individual judgement cannot be trusted. The final arbiter has to be the Body of Christ, because when the Body agrees Heaven acts. This verse confirms that it is right that the Body makes final judgement in these situations and vital that the Body does not allow a wrong done by an individual to go unchallenged. Any disciple who lives under the Lordship of Christ should respect the authority of the Body. This carries the endorsement of Heaven, 'binding and loosing' relates to knowing the right from the wrong. Such divine authority, against which there is no appeal, must be used with care and compassion. Relationships are important, we must get them right.

Verses 19, 20. The third principle formed in this promise gives a whole new perspective to the gathering of the insignificant two or three. The promise gives authority to the prayers offered on behalf of the sinner in the previous verses. The principle of the presence of Jesus is of utmost significance. The prayer is impotent if it is not compatible with the one in whose name it is offered. This means that prayer can never be self-motivated. It means we are not to seek confirmation of answers we already have, but insight and authority from the Lord. It is His will not mine, that must count here. The promise of presence operates in two spheres; in the sphere of the Church wherever the faithful meet, however few or many; also in the sphere of appropriate action. When the Body deals with broken relationships, the two or three must be accompanied by the one. It is always two plus one! three plus one! Prayer is impotent and reconciliation impossible without His promised presence. His presence stops us seeking confirmation of our own judgements, but brings by His presence the insight, purpose and authority of heaven.

5: WHO'S COUNTING? (21–35)

If we needed any further persuasion concerning the seriousness of maintaining the unity of the Body, Matthew concludes this teaching with Peter's question. We owe a great deal to Peter who is never afraid to ask the right question. Peter thought he was being very generous. The Jewish law said, forgive three times, Peter was offering seven times. (Seven was the perfect number.) Jesus replies with His 'seventy-times-seven' which is an impossible number, perhaps suggesting that true forgiveness was made possible only in Him, and that true forgiveness has no limit at all. The reason for this unlimited forgiveness is explained through the parable.

There is an unthinkable difference between the debt owed by the first servant and the second. The King's response not to defer the debt but to cancel it out, goes far beyond what was asked. It emphasises the undeserved basis of God's forgiveness. The conclusion of the parable is that those who refuse to forgive will not be forgiven. Divine and human forgiveness go hand in hand. The size of the debt is so great we can never repay it. He asked for a loan and received a blessing beyond calculation. Nothing we can do to each other can compare with what we have done to God. If God has forgiven us what we owe Him; nothing we have to forgive others could faintly or remotely compare with what we have been forgiven. We never really know what Grace is. We do not understand clearly what the Gospel is. Our tendency is to say to God, "what we cannot do today, we will do later on." How absurd for the servant to plead for time. "Give me time. My intentions are good." In the operation of Grace there is no hope of repayment and none expected. God always gives more than we ask or think. That is Grace. But God has a purpose in being gracious to us. All who receive Grace must learn the outworking of Grace. God expects us to become Gracious. We read this parable and feel anger toward the person who refuses to pass on the same measure he has received. He was right to demand payment! But our life in Christ is based not on rightness but graciousness.

> "Not the labour of my hands
> Can fulfil thy law's demands;
> Could my zeal no respite know,
> Could my tears forever flow,
> All for sin could not atone."

A forgiving spirit is the fruit of a forgiven soul. Personal forgiveness of another individual can never be withheld.

Verse 35: Draws the conclusion "From your heart." Often we forgive from our face, by our lips, or even through our actions, but do not forgive from the heart. Standing on this teaching, we shall be saved from many errors. God has demonstrated through Jesus how we should get along together. Now, with His help we are expected to show family likeness in the way we get along together.

QUESTIONS

1: How do you think the Kingdom of God differs from this world?

2: Become as a child "Not a trait of character but a change in position" Phil. 2, 1 Cor. 3:1. What is meant here?

3: Share examples of how we trip each other up.

4: Our behaviour in the world can cause others to fall. What is our responsibility here?

5: What is your faith worth to you?

6: "Those damaging the Body should be rooted out and cast away!" Can love fail to follow this teaching?

7: The parable of the stray sheep shows the importance of the 'one'. What does this mean for us today?

8: We must not ignore the fault of others - 1 Cor. 9:9–22. 1 Peter 3:1. Is it our business?

9: Matthew lays down a procedure for restoration that carries the endorsement of heaven in 'binding and loosing'. What would this mean for our Church?

10: 'Where two or three gather together'. How have we seen this promise and what should it say of small being big?

11: Righteousness or Grace. What is the difference?

12: The parable of the servants shows our position before God. What do you think your position is?

5. CONFIDENCE IN THE POWER OF JESUS Matthew 9

A PRAYER
Dear Lord,
How low you stooped to touch my crippling need.
How great the sacrifice you made to set me free.
Without you Lord I am lost and dead,
And all that this world offers is but dirt and dust.
Bathing in the full sun of your blessing,
I rest my soul and set my face to heaven.
Like the disciples I build my tent
on some rare mountaintop
and settle there to hold your presence.
Open my ears Lord, to hear the cries,
Brothers and sisters who do not know.
Like scattered sheep afraid and lost.
The harvest Lord,
Of countless souls who need your love.
Open my eyes Lord, that I might gaze
Into eyes that look,
but do not see
The beauty of your face.
Or know the wonder of you grace.
Alone and no-one cares;
With sores that no-one tends.
A harvest out of humiliations, despairs and hatreds.
Lord I ask for no love,
But the love that reaches into another's pain.
No search, but the seeking of someone else's peace,
however low or lost.
No greater privilege
Than that of embracing another
With compassion and care.
No joy but the joy of bringing
a brother or sister to you.
So to pray, to love and sacrifice until all are safely
Home, then joy, and peace and Paradise! Amen.

NOT THE HEALTHY BUT THE SICK
INTRODUCTION:
The miracle recorded in these verses is the last in the second set of three miracle stories told by Matthew.

In 8: 23–27 Jesus has authority over creation.

In 8: 28–34 Jesus has authority over spirits.

In 9: 1–8 Jesus has authority to forgive sins.

This has been something Israel believed only God could do.

Psalm 103:12; Isaiah 1:18; 43:25; 55:6–7; Jeremiah 31:34; Micah 7:19.

Matthew uses this story to emphasise that Jesus is the Son of God.

1: A MAT MAKES IT REAL! (1-8)
With this miracle a new stage in the ministry of Jesus begins. Until this point, Jesus was seen as a teacher, a miracle worker and a prophet, but now the full realisation of what He claims begins to dawn on those around Him.

Jesus leaves the region of Gadara on the east shore of Galilee and returns to Capernaum. This is the same story that Marks tells (Mark 2:1) but Matthew has changed the setting. When Jesus and the disciples reach shore, they are met by two men carrying their lame friend on a stretcher. Jesus sees their confidence, a better translation than faith here. This is confidence they have in Him. Miracles do not depend on the size of your faith, they depend on the size of your God. Jesus says to the lame man, "Take heart, son; your sins are forgiven."

There are three points here which are important:

a) The man needed to hear that he was forgiven. To be forgiven was to be accepted. To be accepted is still the best health-giving news a person could receive. So many people have a low sense of self-worth. Society maintains an underclass of failures, those who cannot make the grade, people written off by the rules and regulations created by an elite. The movers and shakers in the Jewish faith, in creating their extensive lists of regulations, created outcasts and failures.

b) Although the representatives of the official religion had taken the doctrine of forgiveness found in the Old Testament, built a whole system of rituals and regulations to secure it, they were totally ignorant of the reality of the experience of forgiveness. The system of religion they had built gave no hope of forgiveness to those most in need of its reality. Our theology is only made credible through experience. The Jews have all the teaching but it has no relevance to the experience of ordinary people.

c) Forgiveness is incomplete without visible evidence. What the leaders contest is, in fact, the counterpart of the same action. To be forgiven is to take up your bed and walk. It is what Wesley called "Fruit meet for repentance." If repentance is real, then what follows should demonstrate the reality of a change. Those who were open-minded knew they had evidenced something unique. To those bound by convention, Jesus was just another blasphemer. Jesus was aware of their thoughts vs. 4–5, (contrast the attitude of the leaders with that of the people in verse 2. He sees their confidence!). For the Jewish leaders, forgiveness was fulfilling a ritual and maintaining strict regulations. People were not forgiven because they did not fulfil the law's requirements as they had defined them. The power of the ministry of Jesus is demonstrated through those people who had no chance of being included because their lifestyle or health excluded them. It was those people Jesus freed and welcomed. When we declare someone's sins forgiven, if they do not get up then their sins are not forgiven. Our ministry is only proved credible through action.

2: WHO CAN BE FORGIVEN AND HOW? (9-13)

The truth that Jesus can forgive sins begs the question; (Levi) who can be forgiven and how? Here Matthew records his own call to discipleship and the feast that followed. He gives his testimony (Mk. 2:13–17; Lk. 5:27–32). As Jesus is leaving Capernaum He sees a man sitting at the tax collector's booth alongside the road. Matthew was most likely a customs official. The main trade route from Syria to Egypt ran through Galilee, and Capernaum acted as a customs station. Matthew owned the tax franchise at what we would call the head office. He paid Herod for the franchise and was allowed to charge what he liked. Hated by many, these customs officers made themselves rich by overcharging. They are always linked in the New Testament with thieves and sinners. There is no mention of Matthew having met Jesus before this encounter, or having any knowledge of Him. For Jesus to call an outcast to follow Him was the greatest sign of acceptance. Such blatant acceptance was a direct confrontation with the religious leaders. He had driven a coach and horses through all that they counted sacred. Matthew lost his comfortable job and found his destiny. He lost a lucrative and secure income and found honour. He lost a settled, comfortable existence and found adventure of the like he had never dreamed of. He left the tax collector's table but took his pen. He left his heritage and gave us an inheritance in his Gospel.

Verse 10: For Jesus to attend a big party in Matthew's house was to present the representatives of the official religion with a breach of every scribal regulation relating to food. Pharisees were fastidious about food preparation. Still today, strict Jews observe rituals of food preparation and cleansing rites.

For Jesus to eat with sinners was a dramatic sign of intimacy and acceptance. The reaction of the leaders was inevitable. Their religion was such that it

43

defined any common Jewish person who could not, or would not, keep the scribal rules of eating, tithing and personal purity; as those who are immoral (Luke 7:37ff) heretics (John 9:16ff) and Gentiles (Gal. 2:15) as well as tax collectors. The leaders quietly drew the disciples aside, questioning why their teacher ate with "irreligious people." They intended, by their quiet gossip, to undermine the disciples' commitment to Jesus.

Jesus overheard their comments and drew attention to the fact that even they had made mistakes:

a) They had not understood the work of the Messiah. They had missed vital clues the prophets had left concerning the Messiah.

b) They had thought righteousness to be only outward and ceremonial, 5:17; 6:18 but they had overlooked the fact that it was relational.

They were more concerned to preserve their own holiness than to help others in need. Still today, for many, salvation is an intensely private and personal thing in which all effort and time is spent in maintaining personal faith without any thought or concern for others.

The Jewish leaders nurtured a ministry of criticism rather than encouragement. They practised a legal goodness that, for the majority of ordinary people, secured condemnation rather than forgiveness and acceptance. They practised a religion which made God theirs through exclusive rituals and rules that secured their elitism and created dependency, rather than offering practical help to the most vulnerable and needy people.

Blinded by their 'institutional structures', they were incapable of recognising God's Grace at work in Matthew's life and missed the miracle of love which made him respond so readily. Jesus came to those whose need was real. In this statement Jesus is not saying that some people were so good that they did not need Him. But it is only those who know how desperately they need Him, who can accept His invitation. Only an unconditional response is accepted.

Verse 13: The difference between Jesus and the religious leaders is found in their conception of what priorities were foremost in the will of God. For the leaders the first priority was obedience to regulation, to keep themselves pure and secure eternal life. Other people were a threat to this purity. For Jesus it is found in His mission to reach desperate people. To reach people, love must stand with them. Two further sayings press this matter home.

a) A quote from Hosea 6:6. A call to reflection: 'Go and learn what this means'. Jesus is referring to Hosea's deep challenge that religion which is external, in which ritual has taken the place of love, is a superficial religion which God deplores.

b) The second comment reflects the shocking effect of 8:11–12. Jesus reverses the standard of the leaders. It is not the righteous who are called; they have been disqualified because of their blind commitment to standards. They considered themselves righteous, not because of the relationship they have with God, but because they have bound themselves to rules and rituals. (Phil. 3:6). Jesus questions the genuineness of their righteousness (5:20; 3:15; 5:6, 10.). Sinners who 'hunger and thirst for righteousness' are closer to true righteousness than the self-satisfied. Desperate hunger and thirst are the real pointers to a living relationship with God, rather than adherence to a system of belief.

3: LEARN ABOUT SKINS AND PATCHES: (14-17)

First, the religious leaders are hostile towards Jesus (Scribes in v 3 and Pharisees in v 11). Now the disciples of John are hostile towards him (11:2; 14:12; Luke 11:1). In Acts 18:25; 19:3 the remnants of John's followers are still around. John 3:25ff; 4:1 suggests that they saw Jesus and His disciples as rivals. They had crystallized all that John stood for and taught, including his teaching and practice of fasting. It was now the doctrine and practice that was held as sacred by them, as the Pharisees held their teaching. They had almost become a denomination. They forgot that John was a forerunner, and they could not move on. History is littered with the fragment followers of great prophets and teachers turning the rubric of faith into sacred text and demanding all should observe it.

Fasting was a regular feature of Old Testament worship. The Pharisees fasted twice a week and now John's disciples fasted as well. However, they have observed that Jesus and His disciples do not. Jesus answers their challenge by referring to a Jewish wedding feast. It is inappropriate for the guests to fast during a wedding feast. The answer of Jesus hints at the coming Messianic banquet (8:11). Already this is anticipated at the table with Matthew and his friends (9:10). Jesus is the bridegroom 25:1ff. Now is a time of joy. Joy does not last forever! It is already true for John's disciples; it will be so for the disciples of Jesus! The challenge here is to take up the cross. It is joy in the shadow of the cross. We see the courage of Jesus. He knew the cross lay ahead.

Verses 16, 17. It must have been a well-known fact that containers made of new skins would give as the wine fermented. Putting new wine into old wineskins was to put wine that would expand into skins that could not expand and so burst. It was also common knowledge that using a new piece of material to patch an old garment never works. The new material simply does more damage to an old garment.

Using the question about fasting as an example, Jesus makes it clear that what He brings is so new that all the old rituals and traditions cannot hold it.

The Jews were passionately attached to things as they were. The law was to them God's last and final word. There comes a time when you cannot patch up that favourite old garment anymore. You need a new one. The followers of Jesus must have the capacity of mind to receive new ideas and live by new principles. Here Jesus is demonstrating again that life in Him cannot ever be constrained by a rigid devotion to ritual and rite. Feasting or fasting, the disciple must radiate an intimate and real walk with God and reflect His influence on their lives. Discipleship is no longer a matter of correct procedure but of living interaction, God's working presence with us in everyday living.

4: WHEN FAITH AND POWER MEET: (18-26)

Here we begin a third series of miracles. These are very important stories which emphasise confidence. We are told that some people are not healed because they don't have enough faith. Having enough faith has never been an issue in the ministry of Jesus. The issue here is, not the size of your faith but, where you place that faith. What is important is not having a big faith, but knowing a big God. 18–26: Matthew shares with us the double healing of Jairus's daughter and the woman with chronic bleeding. That this important Jewish leader came to Jesus shows how desperate he must have been.

On the way to the ruler's house a woman, suffering for twelve years from chronic bleeding, comes up behind Jesus, trying to touch the tassels on His robe. She has confidence that if she can only touch a tassel she would be healed. On succeeding, she is petrified as Jesus turns round asking "who touched me?" The woman stands forward and owns up. Jesus then says, "Cheer up; your confidence in Me has brought you healing." The tense suggests she was healed even before Jesus spoke. However, it was the presence and power of Jesus, not the measure of her faith which healed her. I have often heard a medical doctor say to a patient, "Put yourself completely in my hands." This woman put all her confidence in the ability of Jesus to heal her. Faith (confidence) plays the pivotal role in the release of Divine activity. The reward of her confidence in Jesus? – She is cured instantly and completely. It is the personal response of Jesus to her personal faith. As she stands on the promise, the blessing she receives is out of all proportion to her faith.

Following this miracle within a miracle, Jesus goes on to the house of the Jewish ruler. On arrival they meet professional mourners, including flute players. Already the ritual has kicked in to mourn the death of the child.

Vs. 23–26. Jesus orders everyone to leave, telling them that she is sleeping rather than dead. They all laugh at Him. Jesus seems to suggest that official religion serves the dead better than the living. They appear to offer no encouragement to the living except the service of mourning at their death. Their religious system has become dislodged from its relationship with God. Christ's mission is to heal, not to bury. The words 'Go away' banishes despair and reflects the hope that Christ brings. There is a contrast shown in this miracle between the cause and effect of institutional religion and the living faith which discerns the purpose of God. Jesus took the stance He took because He was in tune with the purpose of God. Institution would claim threescore years and ten for every individual. Living faith discerns what God's purpose is for the individual and allows God to be sovereign.

5: HAMMER HOME THE POINT: (27-35)

These two blind men had heard enough about Jesus to be sure that He was the promised King and could help them. Their appeal for mercy is an emotional and desperate cry for help. The men know that the response they hope to get from Jesus is not deserved. However, the response of Jesus is anything but emotional. It is a practical love responding to a desperate need. It is a right action in response to a real need. Here, as in all other cases, faith is challenged and tested. Faith, here as in every other incident, is a practical confidence in the power of Jesus. Here, as elsewhere, the deed matches the faith (confidence).

Verses 32–34: The dumb man healed: This miracle leaves us in no doubt that there are only two responses to the authority of Jesus. It provokes either wonder or opposition. The comment in verse 33 is an indictment against a religious leadership that has failed to represent God's compassion or reflect His power. It is a real contrast between the authority of Jesus and that of the religious leaders. His actions demonstrated the 'breaking in' of the Kingdom of God. The leaders could not deny the facts, but they refused the interpretation. They knew Isaiah 35:3–5 and could see it happening in front of them, but they refused to accept it. What was happening was alien to all that they had been taught to expect. They were too set in their ways. They were too proud to submit. They were too prejudiced to see. It is the person with a desperate and deep sense of need who always sees Jesus as the truth and power of God. The person who is prejudiced, proud, and self-righteous cannot submit. They will resist, resent and hate, and in the end seek to eliminate Him. The real need here is not seen in the deaf and dumb man but the religious leaders. They are the real deaf and dumb in Israel.

The ruler came to Jesus, confident that Jesus could heal the dying. The woman came to Jesus with confidence even in her hopelessness. The blind men came, confident that He could give them sight. The dumb man was confident Jesus could free his voice. All found His love and power waiting for them. It does not matter how you come to Christ, or what your need is, that you come is what matters. You have no right to criticise another's motives, or their grasp of theology. In the light of the Kingdom, it is only your confidence in Christ that matters.

6: THE TASK AND RESOURCES: (35-38)

In these verses Matthew makes clear the three-fold ministry of Master and disciple alike: teaching, preaching and healing. When Jesus sees the needs of the many people who come to Him, He feels compassion towards them. 'Compassion' literally means gut reaction. The phrase 'sheep without a shepherd' (Ez. 34:5; 1 Kings 22:17) relates to those lacking spiritual care and guidance. 'Harassed and helpless' literally means torn and thrown away. It can mean skinned, those who are completely worn out, exhausted, scattered, thrown down in an utterly helpless and forsaken condition. They are unprotected from predators, abused by uncaring shepherds. This description relates to the ordinary people of Israel. They are lost sheep 10:6; 15:24; Ezek 34:23; Mi. 5:4. These are the ones that the system had failed.

Verses 37, 38. Jesus is troubled, not only because of the greatness of the need and the lack of resources, but because of the urgency of the situation. Urgency and opportunity are two great Kingdom themes. The harvest refers to people's readiness to respond to the Gospel. Often we see only the surface things in another's life and conclude that they are beyond help or not ready to listen, incapable of responding to the Good News. It was true then, as it is now, that if you were to ask the person out on the street about the Church, they would tell you they were not interested. Ask, then as now, of their spiritual needs and you find a people hungry and desperate for God. Jesus describes a vast field of wheat which demands immediate action, or else it will be destroyed, and a large number of workers are needed to harvest it. He sees the crowd as such a harvest with very few trying to reap it.

Amy Carmichael tells of a dream in which she is standing on a grassy bank leading down to a cliff edge. Thousands of people are walking down the slope and falling over the edge of the cliff. She spends her time desperately rushing back and forth turning as many people as she can around to face away from the edge and certain death. Taking a breath, she noticed, under the shade of a large tree, a group of people having a picnic, oblivious to the cries of those falling to their death. Jesus gives every disciple an important task to do. Pray! This is not simply a call to inactivity, but to action that is being immersed in fervent prayer. Only God is able to provide the necessary resources to complete the task. The call of Christ is for every Christian to be a missionary, a labourer in the field. If the harvest is ever to be reaped, then every believer has to be a reaper. There is someone each and every disciple must bring to God. The demand of the Kingdom is that each of us looks, sees and lends a hand. Sometimes we see only the surface life of other people and conclude that they are hopeless cases. Ask of their need and they are desperate for God. Sometimes we consider the vast size of the task and think our effort is wasted.

God make me willing to be the answer to the prayer I pray for those around me. We pray "Oh that they may see Jesus!" I want to cry "In me!" "In ME!" For if God cannot change the one who prays, how can He change the one who is prayed for? How can we ever expect God to send out others if we ourselves are not prepared to be sent out too?

QUESTIONS

1: The Church is the only organisation that exists for those who are not its members. Does this chapter give you clues to help us in our attitude and outreach?

2: Is it possible to know the doctrine and ceremony of the Church, but not the reality of Jesus?

3: Fasting or feasting? Old garment, new patch!
What do these scriptures say to you today?

4: We are challenged to make an unconditional response to Jesus.
What conditions do you put on your response?

5: How open are you to what God wants to do?

6: Faith releases Divine activity! What does this mean for you?

7: How would you describe the 'harvest field'?

8: Are we good shepherds of the flock? Who are your flock?

9: What do you consider harvesting to be today?

10: How do you think non-Christians see us?

11: What kind of miracles do you expect from God?

11: Every disciple a missionary! What about you?

6. HEARING WITHOUT DOING = DISASTER!
Matthew 7

A PRAYER
Dear Lord,
Why do I find it so easy?
That word of spiteful criticism which gained
nothing for me, and hurt another so much?
I find it so easy to find fault in others.
That harsh, self-righteous comment,
devoid of both love and mercy;
By which I forfeit my place in Your Kingdom.
Why do I find it easier to see another's weakness
Than to recognise my own?
Your standard is set so high Lord, and
there are so many conflicting voices,
each claiming to be the true way, the real life.
You have called me to the sweet restrictions of love;
Yet I find more company in wrong doing.
I wear the outer garments of the Gospel
but my inner being seeps out its wrongs.
I am afraid Lord, that when I have done all,
Said all, seen all, and calling Lord! Lord!
You will not answer me.
With all my well dressed faith
I look for your recognition
and find none.
Lord, keep me asking, seeking, knocking,
alert to hear your words of life.
Knowing that I am not yours by hearing,
Give me strength to do all that you command.
That in my journeying,
I might respond to your prompting,
And at my arriving,
you might respond to my calling.
Amen.

INTRODUCTION:
In this Chapter Matthew presents Jesus standing solidly against criticism which is spiteful, uncaring and hypocritical. He warns people against bad

decisions, false informers and superficial evidence. True discipleship is built on preparation, forethought and sound foundation. Hearing God's word and not obeying it is to invite disaster.

1: WATCH YOUR ATTITUDE (1-12)

Within the teaching of the early Church it was necessary for Christians to make very careful value judgements, as in vs. 6 and 15-20 of this chapter. There is a process for dealing with those who wrong you, first through direct challenge and, if that fails, by taking progressively stronger measures: 18:15-17. This passage, however, is concerned with fault-finding, condemnation of another's failings combined with a blindness to see your own. It is a picture of harsh self-righteous criticism of another individual which shows neither love nor mercy. Blind to your own shortcomings you seem unaware that it is a member of the Body of Christ that you criticize. Habitual critics forfeit their citizenship in the Kingdom. The least that such an attitude can expect is to be judged by the same harshness that it affords the other person.

Why are disciples commanded not to judge?
a)   Because we never know the whole facts of the situation.
b)   Because we can never be strictly impartial.
c)   Because we are never good enough to have the right to judge.

Sorting out our own lives is hard enough to do. It takes all our energy concentrating on our own faults; better to leave the faults of others to God.

This graphic illustration from the Carpenter's Joke Book, exposes dramatically the hypocrisy of judging others while failing to address faults in ourselves. The tiny splinter (*karphos*) = something in your eye so minute that you feel the pain, but is very difficult to see and deal with. However, the log, literally a beam or rafter, something that is so outrageously huge, so obvious that it is farce-like in its appearance, should be the easiest to see and deal with.

This teaching clearly condemns inconsistency. It is not the diagnosis which is wrong, the splinter is no less painful or wrong, but the failure to apply the same standard to yourself as others. Contrary to what many think, Christian Discipleship does not demand that I centre my efforts directly on other people. As with the telescope, the disciple is to focus on the other person through two lenses. The one is Christ and the other is self. These two lenses prevent me from judging others. I focus on those around me through the uniqueness of Christ and knowledge of myself in relation to Him. I can only approach others through Christ. It must always be me and Christ and the other person.

7:6. This was a saying used in two ways in the early Church.
a)   Used by those who thought God's Grace was only for the Jews. These

were the people Paul clashed with on his missionary journeys. This is a text which can be used and abused easily.

b)   The early Church was under threat both from outside and within.

There were those who would compromise between Christian and pagan thought, to get a belief which all could be happy with. If the Christian Church was to survive, it had to defend itself. The main threat was in the temptation to become just another of the many religions which competed within the Roman Empire. This text was used to maintain the purity of the faith necessary if Christianity was not to drown in a sea of paganism. This was especially so in relation to the Lord's Supper. In all these ways the text is used to support exclusiveness.

This verse is supposed to be a 'parallelism' already seen in Matthew 6: 10. Just one word wrong and the saying does not work. Holy does not balance with pearls. However, the Hebrew for holy (KDSH) is the same as the Aramaic for earring (KDSH). Again there is something of the humour of Jesus shining through here. The image is of a pearl earring in a sow's ear! It is something completely out of place, incongruous. The original could have run 'Don't give earrings to the dogs; or pearl earrings to swine.' Now the parallelism is perfect. If this is right it would mean that there are some people who are not fit, not able, to receive the message which the Church is so willing to give. It is not a statement of exclusiveness, but a statement of practical difficulty in communication, which meets the missioner of every generation. There are some people with whom you cannot share faith. Something has to happen to them in order for them to be receptive. It may be that their minds are shut; or brutalised; it may be that they have absolutely no common ground on which we can communicate. It is sometimes impossible to talk to some people about Jesus. Their insensitiveness, moral blindness, intellectual pride, cynical mockery, make them impervious to any words about Christ. But it is always possible to show them Jesus. The weakness of the Church is not its shortage of argument, but its shortage of truly Christ-like examples.

7–12: The standards set for real disciples are very high. However, help is available from the Father. What the disciple is unable to do, the Father can enable them to do. The disciple is to 'ask, seek and knock'. Everyone who seeks such help will receive it. All three words are imperatives in the present tense and relate to prayer. Go on asking, go on seeking, go on knocking. It requires constant, continuous and persistent prayer if it is to be answered. God will provide nothing of the inferior substitute or indeed anything that will hurt or harm the disciple. God will always answer prayer in His way, through wisdom and love. It is your prayer life which tests the rightness of the thing you pray for and tests your sincerity in asking for it.

Verse 12: This verse acts as a conclusion for 7:1-11. A true disciple's actions toward others will be governed by how much the disciple loves himself or herself. To obey this commandment, a person must become a new creation with a new Centre to life. If the world was peopled by these new creations, it would be a new world.

2: CONTRASTS (13–23)

The radical demands of Jesus have been expressed in the main body of teaching (Ch. 1–5) climaxing in the all-embracing principle of 7:12. Each of the next sections 13–14; 15–20; 24–27 gives us a contrast between the genuine and the false. The genuine is found, not in the disciple's profession of faith, but in their performance, **13 – 14.** The idea of life here is paralleled with entering the Kingdom (v.21). This is a matter for a definite and deliberate decision. Real discipleship is a minority religion. The words 'easy and hard' are not good translations. Better translate *euruchoros* (easy) = roomy and *tethlimmene* (hard) = restricted. This relates to popularity rather than a comfortable journey. It is the way that is not very popular and only interests a few because it demands decision and sacrifice.

'Life' refers to two things.
- a) Blessings of the coming age.
- b) Truly fulfilled life here and now.

Christian discipleship offers fullness of life which does not tarnish. The broad way encourages indecision, but brings self-satisfaction. However, it is the way that leads to destruction, offering short term pleasure, which tarnishes, and brings long-term loss that is ultimate.

Verses 15–20: Prophecy is an honoured gift in the New Testament Church (Acts 11:27–28, 21:9-11; 1 Cor. 12: 10, 28:14ff.) False prophets offer an easier alternative to the narrow way of Christian discipleship. The disciple has to know the difference between the restricted and the roomy way.

The long and short way; the things that last never happen quickly. The disciplined and undisciplined way; there can be no progress without discipline.

There are thoughtful and thoughtless ways. The only way to get our values right is to see, not short term, but long term values. False teachers are not easily detected. They may look like sheep (disciples are often called sheep) but in fact they are in disguise and much more to be feared. They bring destruction, not simply to the single sheep but to the whole flock. How can I detect false teachers? 'By their fruits' (v.16) points to an external rightness. They draw attention to themselves with a tendency to exalt men and women, not to seek God's mercy and grace.

Their basic fault is self-interest.

They teach solely for self-gain.
They teach solely for self-prestige.
They teach solely to transmit their own ideas.

The true prophets listen to God before they speak. They never forget that they are nothing more than a voice to speak for God. A channel through which God's Grace can flow. Never pushing their own ideas of truth, but only the truth as it is in Jesus Christ.

a) Teaching is false if it leads to over emphasis on keeping rules and regulations. False teachers tend to do three things.
b) They produce an easy religion.
c) They divorce belief from life.
d) They have an attitude that is arrogant and separatist.

Verses 21–23: In these three verses we face the ultimate rejection of superficial discipleship. The first group in vs.1-6 were responsible for deluding others, here we face those who are self-deluded. In these verses it is ordinary believers who are mentioned. These people think they have the right qualifications to guarantee them a place in the Kingdom. They point to the orthodoxy of their belief, their zeal and spiritual gifts (prophecy, driving out demons). None of these are denied, but the thing which is missing is v.21, "doing the will of my Father who is in Heaven." Charismatic activity is no substitute for obedience to and personal relationship with Jesus. Nor are any other good works. You are judged by your relationship with Jesus. We still need to learn that it is possible to be orthodox, fervent, useful and gifted and yet, without a Godly character and life, never to be a real disciple, never knowing or being known by God in Jesus. Nobody can ultimately deceive God who sees the truth about each of us.

3: BUILDERS BE CAREFUL (24–27)
This well-known parable of the builders serves here to show that it is not in the hearing that the two builders differ but in the doing. *'Poieo'* 'to do' is a key word in all these three sections. Your ability to survive depends on your practical response to Jesus. Only the life whose foundations are sure can stand the test. Jesus demands two things:
a) That people should listen. Hear what Jesus says!
b) That people should do. Knowledge is only good if it is acted on. Theory without practice is dead. To be a real disciple is to hear and do. The word 'GREAT' highlights the seriousness of this truth. Hearing and doing is the only safe way to secure your life against all that will seek to undermine your commitment to Jesus.

4: HE REALLY MEANS IT! (28–29)

Matthew records that they were amazed at the authority of Jesus.

a) It was not the way in which Jesus said things, but what He said in His teaching which had authority. Jesus claimed things which could be true only of God (7:21, 24, 21–23).

b) Jesus completely denied that anyone could make themselves acceptable to God by their own effort alone. This teaching was the complete opposite of all that the Pharisees and religious leaders had taught.

c) Jesus demanded that obedience to God has to be real, not simply a routine response to rule or ritual as was the response of the teachers of the law.

QUESTIONS

1: Constructive criticism. How does this differ from what Matthew is marking out in this passage? How do you deal with habitual critics?

2: How would you respond to a Church member, or non Church member, who thinks they are doing all that is required in verse 12? What do you make of the splinter and log illustration on inconsistency?

3: Threats from outside and threats from within. What is the threat of compromise? How serious is it? What false teaching do you see in the Church today? Is Christianity in danger of becoming just another religion?

4: If there are those who are unable to receive the Good News, how do I get to, and identify, those who are receptive?

5: How does your Church assess the genuineness of those who claim to be Christian? What would you consider practical difficulties?

6: Is the weakness of the Church not a shortage of argument but a shortage of truly Christian lives?

7: "Those damaging the 'Body' should be rooted out and cast away!" Can love fail to follow this teaching?

8: Ask! Seek! Knock! What does this mean for you today?

9: You can trust God never to give bad things to us! Do you?

10: It is not profession which counts but performance. What does this mean in real terms?

11: Wide and Narrow! Roomy and restricted! Do you understand what Jesus is getting at here?

12: How can you detect false teachers? What should you do? Think about the right qualifications (vs.21–23).

Look out for

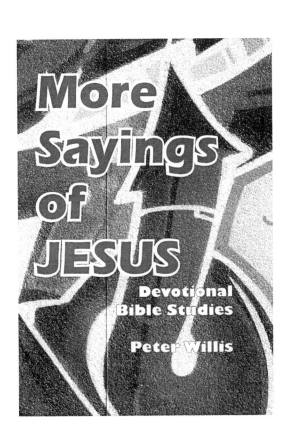

We are growing publishers, adding several new titles to our list each year. We also undertake private publications and commissioned works.

Our range includes:-

Books of Verse:
Devotional Poetry
Recitations for Children
Humorous Monologues

Drama
Bible Plays
Sketches
Christmas, Passiontide,
Easter and Harvest Plays
Demonstrations

Resource Books
Assembly Material
Songs and Musicals
Children's Addresses
Prayers
Worship and Preaching
Books for Speakers

Activity Books
Quizzes
Puzzles

Church Stationery
Notice Books
Cradle Roll Certificates
Presentation Labels

Associated Lists and Imprints
Cliff College Publishing
Nimbus Press
Headway
Social Work Christian Fellowship

Please send a stamped addressed envelope (C5 approx 9" x 6") for the current catalogue or consult your local Christian Bookshop who will either stock or be able to obtain Moorleys titles.